perspective

The last two years have been a great adventure. I left the rural beauty of my home in the Comox Valley on the west coast of Canada, and travelled east seeking new experiences.

When I arrived in London, I had no idea where I would end up. Over the course of my life I have lived in many cities: Vancouver, Toronto, San Francisco, Montreal, Rome, Merida and Bremen. At this turning point, I knew that I wanted to experience life in a European city once again. I travelled by train through several English cities, taking in the flavour of the countryside and imagining what my life might be like in London, York, or Manchester. Edinburgh was the final stop on my train tour, and I was entranced by the architecture, views, and scale of the city. I immediately felt that this was the place for me.

Since my arrival I have explored the city and countryside and enjoyed the frenetic party atmosphere of two Edinburgh festival seasons.

My impressions of Scotland and England are coloured by my perspective as a foreigner, as I often compare life here to my experiences of life in Canada and the US. Discovering the subtle differences in culture, lifestyle, and landscape is a pleasure and a constant inspiration.

Handmade in the UK is an aesthetic response to my new home, and also an introduction to the local community of dyers and yarn producers. Each design features a unique yarn that has passed through the hands of a hard-working local artisan. The subtle colour variations in these exquisite yarns add depth and beauty to the lace designs.

contents

BONNY ::: p8 ::: shell
10 sizes: ladies XXS to 4XL
yarn: lace weight alpaca / silk

LUSH ::: p20 ::: cardigan
16 sizes: 0-6 months to ladies 4XL
yarn: DK or worsted weight wool

WINDSWEPT ::: p38 ::: pullover
16 sizes: 0-6 months to ladies 4XL
yarn: DK weight wool / angora

WINDING WAY ::: p6 ::: socks
3 sizes: adult S, M, L
yarn: superwash BFL 4-ply

LOCH ::: p32 ::: hat + mittens
5 sizes: baby to adult large
yarn: sport weight cashmere

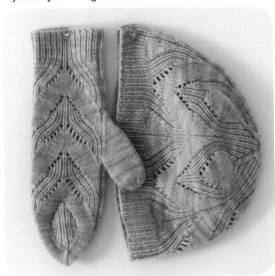

ROSEWATER ::: p14 ::: beret
5 sizes: baby to adult large
yarn: DK weight wool / alpaca blend

ESTUARY ::: **p28** ::: shawl
1 size; adjustable
yarn: 4-ply superwash merino

THISTLE ::: **p26** ::: stole / scarf
one size; adjustable
yarn: 4-ply wool / alpaca blend

BOTANY ::: **p16** ::: shawl
2 sizes: small, large
yarn: 4-ply angora blend

VIVID ::: **p4** ::: blanket
size as desired *(sample is baby blanket size)*
yarn: as desired *(sample in 4-ply wool)*

the romantic city

I was raised in Canada, and for me historic cities have an underlying beauty and romance. Layers of history seem to imbue the stone walls and cobbled streets with a level of meaning that goes beyond day-to-day reality.

Edinburgh has historically been an important centre of culture, art, and philosophical thought and was known as 'the Athens of the North' in the 18th century. The city is full of universities, libraries, students, and artists, and it is an invigorating place to live.

In this romantic city I have crafted a new life for myself. The beauty of my surroundings inspires me every day, and for some indefinable reason living in this city makes me feel that my life is full of immense possibility.

WINDING WAY

The medieval centre of Edinburgh is constructed on a hill crowned by a fairy-tale castle. Dozens of stone staircases enclosed in narrow passageways ascend the hill.

These staircases inspired the lace panel which decorates these simple socks.

sizing: Adult Small (Medium, Large)
Circumference: 7.5 (8, 8.5) inches
Length: Adjustable

materials:

Yarn: 360 (380, 400) yds sock weight yarn (*sample shown in **Old Maiden Aunt Bluefaced Leicester 4ply** in 'buttermint'*)

Gauge: 30 sts & 44 rows / 4" in stockinette stitch

Needles: US #1 / 2.25 mm (*or as req'd to meet gauge*) double pointed needles

Notions: stitch markers, darning needle

pattern: These socks are knit from cuff to toe.

CO 57 (60, 63) sts, PM and join for working in the round. Establish ribbing: (k2, p1) around. Work 1.5 inches in ribbing as established.

Setup Round: k1, m1, k13, PM, p1, (k2, p1) to end [58 (61, 64) sts]

Establish lace pattern: For first sock, work chart beginning on round 1, for a mirrored second sock, work chart beginning on round 21.

Round 1: work chart A (15 sts), p1, (k2, p1) to end
Round 2: k15, p1, (k2, p1) to end

Continue as established, working from chart until leg of sock measures 6.5 inches *(or desired length)*, ending with an odd # round *(for sample, I worked rounds 1-40, then worked 1-19 once more)*.

Next Round: Work in pattern, stopping 6 (7, 9) sts before end of round.

heel flap: Turn work so WS is facing.

Next Row (WS): sl1, p30, place remaining 27 (30, 33) sts on hold. You will now work back in forth in rows on these 31 sts to form the heel flap.

Row 1 (RS): sl1, (k1, sl1) to last 2, k2
Row 2 (WS): sl1, purl to end
Work rows 1-2 a total of 15 (16, 17) times.

heel turn: You will use short-rows to turn heel.

Row 1 (RS): sl1, k17, ssk, k1, turn work
Row 2 (WS): sl1, p6, p2tog, p1, turn work
Row 3: sl1, knit to 1 st before gap, ssk (to close gap), k1, turn
Row 4: sl1, purl to 1 st before gap, p2tog (to close gap), p1, turn

Repeat rows 3-4 until all sts have been worked. [19 sts remain]

gusset: BOR (beginning of round) from this point forward is located at start of heel sts.

Round 1: sl1, k18 *(heel sts)*, pick up 16 (17, 18) sts along edge of heel flap, PM, work in ribbing and lace pattern as established across top of foot, PM, pick up 16 (17, 18) sts along edge of heel flap. [78 (83, 88) sts]

Round 2: k19 *(heel sts)*, k-tbl to marker, work in pattern across top of foot to marker, k-tbl to end.

Round 3: knit to 2 sts before marker, k2tog, work in pattern across top of foot to marker, ssk, knit to end

Round 4: knit to marker, work in pattern across top of foot to marker, knit to end

Work rows 3-4 a total of 10 (11, 12) times. [58 (61, 64) sts]

foot: Work in rounds, continuing in pattern as set at top of foot, and stockinette stitch around the bottom. Work until foot measures 6.5 (7, 7.5) inches from heel, or 1.5 inches short of desired length.

toe: **Setup Round:** work instructions for your size.

Small: Remove BOR marker, k24, replace marker for new BOR. K29, PM, knit to end. [58 sts]
Medium: Remove BOR marker, k25, replace marker for new BOR. K30, PM, ssk, knit to end. [60 sts]
Large: Remove BOR marker, k26, replace maker for new BOR. K32, PM, knit to end. [64 sts]

Round 1: [k1, ssk, knit to 3 sts before marker, k2tog, k1] twice
Round 2: knit
Work rounds 1-2 a total of 8 (9, 9) times. [26 (24, 28) sts]

Use Kitchener stitch to graft toe closed. Work second sock same as first, or to work a mirrored pair, start lace pattern on round 21 as noted.

finishing: Weave in all ends, and block your socks.

---

chart A - repeat rounds 1-40

start second sock on round 21

← 15 stitch panel →

key & abbreviations

☐ **k** - knit

⊙ **yo** - yarn over

⟋ **k2tog** - knit 2 sts together

⟍ **ssk** - slip 2 stitches knitwise (one at a time), then knit 2 slipped stitches together through back loops

chart notes

Charts represent odd number rounds only.
All even number rounds: knit.
Charts are worked from right to left.
For first sock, begin on chart round 1. For a mirrored second sock, begin on chart round 21.

Cassy (33" bust) is wearing size S (32.5") which is 0.5 inches positive ease. For comparison, see photo on page 11 to see how this garment fits with negative ease.

materials:

Yarn: lace weight yarn: **see table for yardage** *(sample in **Juno Fibre Arts Alice Lace** in 'duck egg').* Bonny may be knit in heavier (sock, sport, DK) weight yarn for a slightly different effect *(yardage will vary).*

Gauge: 22 sts and 34 rows / 4" in stockinette *For a proper fit it is crucial to make a large swatch and block it to determine your blocked stitch and row gauge.*

Needles: US #4 / 3.5 mm 24 inch circular

Notions: stitch markers, darning needle

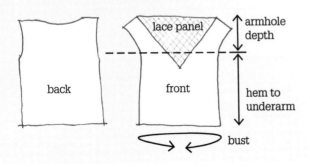

sizing: Pattern includes 10 adult sizes:

Size	Bust	Armhole depth	Hem to UA	Yardage
XXS	28"	6.5"	14"	600
XS	30"	6.75"	14"	650
S	32.5"	7"	15"	700
M	34.5"	7.5"	16"	750
ML	36"	7.75"	16.5"	800
L	39"	8"	17"	850
XL	43"	8.5"	17"	900
XXL	46"	8.75"	17.5"	1000
3XL	50"	9"	18"	1100
4XL	54"	9"	18"	1200

Finished garment measurements given; choose a size based upon your measurement + desired ease.

sizing notes: Choose a size 1 to 4 inches smaller than your bust measurement, as the fabric is extremely stretchy, and it should cling over bust. If working garment in a heavier yarn the fabric will be less stretchy, so choose a size with less negative ease. Garment is shown on 2 models for comparison.

BONNY

This simple yet dramatic lace shell is perfect for an elegant night out, summer garden party, or Sunday afternoon stroll through the city.

The lace triangle with a crisp geometric pattern adds interest and form to the top while maintaining the classic simplicity.

pattern: Bonny is knit in the round from hem to underarm, then in rows to complete front and back.

body: Cast on 154 (166, 178, 190, 198, **218, 234, 254, 274, 294**) sts loosely, PM and join for working in the round. Work in stockinette stitch (knit all rounds).

Work in rounds until the fabric, *after blocking*, will measure 11 (11, 12, 13, 13, **13.5, 13.5, 14, 14, 14**) inches in *YOUR* row gauge. If you achieved the row gauge stated (8.5 rows / inch), work a total of 94 (94, 102, 110, 110, **114, 114, 120, 120, 120**) rounds.

Establish lace panel at front of shell:

Round 1: knit 36 (39, 42, 45, 47, **52, 56, 61, 66, 71**), work row 1 of chart A over next 5 sts, knit 36 (39, 42, 45, 47, **52, 56, 61, 66, 71**), PM *(R underarm)*, knit to end

Round 2 and following even number rounds: knit

Continue as established, working lace panel at center front. As lace panel sts increase, the stockinette stitches each side decrease and the total stitch count remains the same.

Work setup rows 3-10 of chart A once.

Work rows 1-12 of chart B once. The total stitch count remains the same, but after row 12 is completed, there are 25 lace panel sts.

Work chart B rows 1 to 2 (2, 4, 4, 6, **6, 8, 8, 10, 10**) one more time; or until there are 27 (27, 29, 29, 31, **31, 33, 33, 35, 35**) lace panel sts. On the last even number round, stop 2 sts before the end of the round.

front: At this point you will split the front and back for working separately (in rows) to the shoulder.

Bind off 4 sts *(2 from back, 2 from front - this is the L underarm)*, ssk, then work across front, working next lace row, to 4 sts before R underarm marker, working k2tog, then placing remaining sts on hold for R underarm and back. Turn work, and purl WS row. [71 (77, 83, 89, 93, **103, 111, 121, 131, 141**) sts]

From this point forward, purl all WS rows, and slip the first stitch of all rows purlwise for a stable edge.

Work 4 (6, 6, 8, 8, **16, 16, 18, 22, 32**) more rows in pattern; or until there are 33 (35, 37, 39, 41, **49, 51, 53, 59, 69**) lace panel sts and 19 (21, 23, 25, 26, **27, 30, 34, 36, 36**) sts in stockinette each side.

From this point continue as established, but work the first and last stitches of the chart as k1 rather than k2tog and ssk. Therefore the stitch count will increase by 2 sts each RS row. In this manner, work a further 52 (54, 56, 58, 52, **56, 56, 56, 56, 46**) rows following pattern; or until the armhole, slightly stretched, measures 6.5 (6.75, 7, 7.5, 7.75, **8, 8.5, 8.75, 9, 9**) inches in depth. [123 (131, 139, 147, 145, **159, 167, 177, 187, 187**) sts]

There are now 85 (89, 93, 97, 93, **105, 107, 109, 115, 115**) sts in the lace panel section. Bind off stockinette stitch sections with a regular bind off and lace using a stretchy bind-off.

Stretchy bind-off: k1, *k1, slip 2 sts back to LH needle and k2tog-tbl, repeat from * to end

Break yarn, leaving a long end for seaming.

back: Put held sts back on needles. With RS facing, attach yarn and bind off 4 sts *(R underarm)*, then work ssk, knit to last 2 sts, k2tog. [71 (77, 83, 89, 93, **103, 111, 121, 131, 141**) sts]

Work in stockinette stitch for the same number of rows as you did for front panel, then bind off.

finishing: block the garment, then sew the stockinette shoulder sections of front to back. The finished size is very dependant on how aggressively the work is blocked; so be gentle for a smaller and stretchier finished item and more aggressive for a larger and more flowing finished piece. If after blocking you find that the armhole depth is too long or short for a perfect fit, simply add or subtract rows at this point before completing the shoulder seams.

Nina (38" bust) is wearing size S (32.5") which is 5.5 inches negative ease. As you can see, the garment is more snug on her than on Cassy, but it still fits nicely. The garment is very stretchy - take this into account when choosing a size.

chart notes

Charts represent odd number rounds (and RS rows) only.
Even number rounds: knit all sts.
WS rows: purl all sts.

Read charts from right to left.

key & abbreviations

k - knit

yo - yarn over

k2tog - knit 2 sts together

ssk - slip 2 stitches knitwise (one at a time), then knit 2 slipped stitches together through back loops

sl1-k2tog-psso - slip 1, k2tog, pass slipped st over

work as k2tog as far as pattern states, then as k1 thereafter

work as ssk as far as pattern states, then as k1 thereafter

chart B - increasing lace panel; repeat rounds 1-12

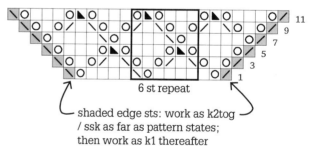

6 st repeat

shaded edge sts: work as k2tog / ssk as far as pattern states; then work as k1 thereafter

chart A - setup - work rounds 1-10

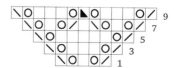

the english garden

The pastoral landscapes of England are lush but well-ordered. Organic lines of hedgerows and stone walls delineate farmland which has been under cultivation for thousands of years.

It is as if the very definition of the word 'picturesque' was created from views of the English pastoral landscape.

This lush botanical richness and soft feminine beauty inspired several floral lace designs with petal and leaf motifs.

ROSE

Hunter is rockin' the toddler size, knit in **Sweet Fiber Avery Sport** in 'charcoal'.

sizing: Baby (Toddler, Child, Adult S/M, Adult L)
Fits head: 16 (18, 20, 22, 24) inches around
samples shown are Adult S/M and toddler

materials:

Yarn: 120 (140, 170, 200, 250) yds DK weight yarn
*(adult S/M sample shown in **The Uncommon Thread Sumptuous DK** in 'breath')*

Gauge: 22 sts / 4" in stockinette st on larger needles

Needles: US #4 / 3.5 mm and US #6 / 4.0 mm
(or as required to meet gauge)
16" circular and double pointed needles

Notions: stitch markers, darning needle

Scotland's most famous architect and artist is Charles Rennie Mackintosh, darling of the art-nouveau movement.

His stylized roses are the inspiration for this original lace stitch pattern.

pattern: Rosewater is knit from brim to crown With smaller needles, CO 76 (76, 90, 106, 120) sts, PM (BOR marker) and join for working in the round.

Establish twisted ribbing: (k1-tbl, p1) around Work in twisted ribbing for 10 (10, 10, 12, 14) rounds. Switch to larger needles.

Increase Round: (k5, m1) to last 6 (6, 0, 6, 0) sts, knit to end.   [90 (90, 108, 126, 144) sts] Knit 1 round.

Following instructions for your size, work lace pattern following charts A and B. The chart notes describe how to move the beginning-of-round (BOR) marker at the start of rounds 9, 13, 15, 19, 21, 23.

Baby Size: Work rows 1-24 of chart A once, then work rows 1-11 of chart B.   [20 sts]

Toddler, Child, Adult S/M: Work rows 1-24 of chart A once, then work rows 1-12 of chart A once more.

NOTE: For Toddler, Child, and Adult S/M: Before working crown decreases you must relocate the BOR marker: remove marker, k9, replace marker.

Work rows 1-11 of chart B.   [- (20, 24, 28, -) sts]

Adult L: Work rows 1-24 of chart A : rosebud lace two times, then work rows 1-11 of chart B : crown decreases.   [32 sts]

All Sizes: Next Round: ssk around.
                                    [10 (10, 12, 14, 16) sts]

Break yarn, leaving a 6 inch tail. Thread tail through remaining sts and pull to close top of hat. Wet-block hat aggressively to reveal lace pattern and achieve desired level of slouchiness.

chart notes

Charts represent odd numbered rounds only. Even numbered rounds: knit all stitches.
Charts are worked from right to left.

It is necessary to relocate BOR marker prior to working rounds marked with arrows as follows:
Rounds 9, 13, 19, 23: shift BOR marker left
Rounds 15 and 21: shift BOR marker right

shifting BOR (beginning of round) marker

← **To shift BOR left:** *prior to working the round remove marker, k1, replace marker.*

→ **To shift BOR right:** *prior to working the round remove marker, slip last st worked (on previous round) from RH to LH needle, replace marker.*

key & abbreviations

☐ **k** - knit

Ⓞ **yo** - yarn over

╱ **k2tog** - knit 2 sts together

╲ **ssk** - slip 2 stitches knitwise (one at a time), then knit 2 slipped stitches together through back loops

◿ **k3tog** - knit 3 sts together

◣ **sssk** - slip 3 stitches knitwise (one at a time), then knit 3 slipped stitches together through back loops

▨ **No Stitch** (inserted for clarity of pattern)

chart B - crown decreases

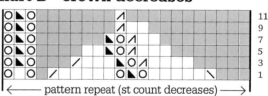

←—— pattern repeat (st count decreases) ——→

11
9
7
5
3
1

chart A - rosebud lace pattern

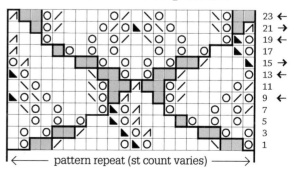

←—— pattern repeat (st count varies) ——→

23 ←
21 →
19 ←
17
15 →
13 ←
11
9 ←
7
5
3
1

The glass houses at Edinburgh's botanical gardens contain a vast array of exotic species, from tiny flowers to massive oversized fronds.

This shawl is inspired by the elegant geometries found within this natural treasure box.

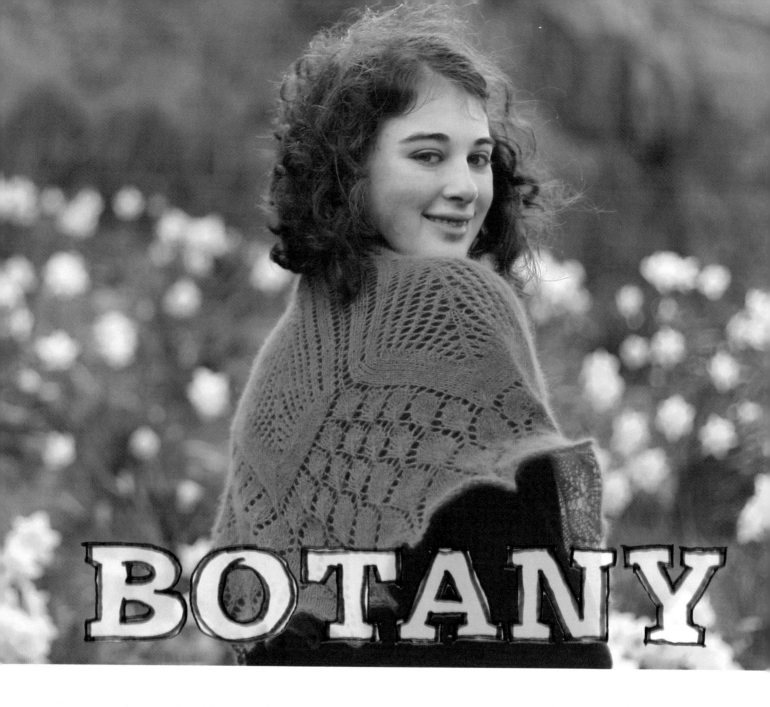

BOTANY

sizing: Small (Large) shawl measures approximately 56 (68) inches wide by 22 (27) inches deep. *Finished size will depend on yarn choice, gauge, and how aggressively you block the finished piece.*

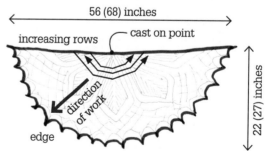

56 (68) inches

increasing rows — cast on point

direction of work

edge

22 (27) inches

materials:

Yarn: 500 (700) yds 4-ply, sock, or DK weight yarn (*small size shawl shown in* **Orkney Angora Aurora 4-ply** *in 'scarlet'*)

Gauge: 22 sts and 27 rows / 4" in stockinette stitch

Needles: US #7 / 4.5 mm; *or as req'd to meet gauge;* 32 inch circular needle

Notions: stitch markers, darning needle

construction: This crescent shawl is worked from the top centre in rows of increasing length to the outer edge. The lace is made by working a series of motifs (these are the large petals), and later by inserting smaller-scale lace panels between these motifs as they decrease to points.

pattern: CO 4 sts **provisionally**. Knit 8 rows.
Next row: knit 4, pick up 4 sts in the edge of the garter stitch rectangle just knit, unpick cast-on, placing 4 sts back on needles, then knit 4 [12 sts].
First WS row: k3, p6, k3

Begin working botanical motifs as follows:

RS rows: k4 (edge), work motif A, work motif B three times, work motif C, k4
WS rows: k3, purl to last 3 sts, k3

You may find it helpful to place markers to indicate start and end of each motif.

Starting Rows (also shown on motif charts A, B, C)
Row 1 (RS): k4, yo, (k1, yo) 4 times, k4
Row 2 and following WS rows: k3, purl to last 3 sts, k3
Row 3: k5, (yo, k1) 8 times, k4
Row 5: k4, ssk, yo, (k1, yo, s2-k1-p2sso, yo) 3 times, k1, yo, k2tog, k4
Row 7: k6, yo, (k1, yo, k3, yo) 3 times, k1, yo, k6

Continue in pattern as established, working rows 8-70 of motif charts A, B and C. [153 sts]

Starting on row 71, charts A, B and C begin to decrease, and you begin to work chart D, which is inserted in between the petals. *The knit sts that separated the motifs flow into / become the start of chart D. Depending on where you have placed markers, you may need to adjust their position on this row.*

Continue working rows 71-90 of motifs A, B, and C, whilst at the same time working rows 1-20 of chart D in the following manner:

RS rows: k4 (edge), work row 71 of motif A, work row 1 of chart D, [work row 71 of motif B, work row 1 of chart D] 3 times, work row 71 of motif C, k4 (edge)
WS rows: k3, purl to last 3 sts, k3
As shown in diagram, the chart order worked on RS rows is now: A, D, B, D, B, D, B, D, C.

Continue in this manner, working rows 3-20 of chart D alongside rows 73-90 of motifs A, B, C. [169 sts]

Repeat chart rows 15-20 of chart D once more alongside rows 91-96 of motifs A, B, C. [177 sts]

Repeat chart rows 15-18 of chart D once more alongside rows 97-100 of motifs A, B, C. [177 sts]

Row 101: k4 (edge sts), ssk (motif A), yo, k1, yo, k2, k2tog, *(k2, yo, k1, yo, k2, sl2-k1-p2sso) four times, k2, yo, sl2-k1-psso (motif B), yo, k2, sl2-k1-psso, repeat from * 2 more times, (k2, yo, k1, yo, k2, sl2-k1-p2sso) three times, k2, yo, k1, yo, k2, ssk, k2, yo, k1, yo, k2tog (motif C), k4 (edge sts) [173 sts]

Now the petal motifs are reduced to a single stitch each and integrated into the lace pattern which spans the entire row. From this point forward work charts D, E, F, G from edge to edge as follows:
RS rows: k5 (edge sts), work chart to last 5 sts, k5
WS rows: k3, purl to last 3 sts, k3

Row 103: k5 (edge sts), work row 15 of chart D, k5
Row 105: k5, work row 17 of chart D, k5 [177 sts]

Work chart E rows 107-116 one time. [229 sts]

Work chart F rows 117-126 one time for small shawl, or 3 times for large shawl. *Note: shaded stitches are worked as k1 on first chart repeat, then as sl2-k1-psso on further chart repeats.* [285 (309) sts]

Work chart G rows 127-128 once, then repeat rows 129-130 three (five) times. [331 (359) sts]

finishing: Bind off all sts using a stretchy bind off method. One that works well is: k1, (k1, place both sts back on LH needle, and k2tog-tbl) repeat to end. Cut yarn and pull through final stitch. Weave in ends, wet block your shawl, and enjoy!

chart G - work rows 127-128 once, then repeat rows 129-130 three (five) times

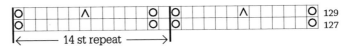

chart F - work rows 117-126 one (three) times

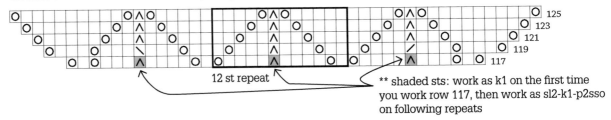

** shaded sts: work as k1 on the first time you work row 117, then work as sl2-k1-p2sso on following repeats

chart E - work rows 107-116 one time

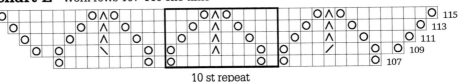

motif A - work at start of row

chart D - work between motifs starting row 71

8 st repeat

motif B - work 3 times each row

note: it is necessary to work row 101 following written instructions

chart notes

Charts show RS rows only.
WS rows: k3, purl to last 3 sts, k3
Charts are read from R to L.
Refer to pattern text for which charts to use in what order.

motif C - work at end of row

key

☐ **k** - knit

○ **yo** - yarn over

╱ **k2tog** - knit 2 together

╲ **ssk** - slip 2 stitches knitwise (one at a time), then knit 2 slipped stitches together through back loops

⋀ **sl2-k1-psso** - slip 2 together, slip 2 together, k1, pass 2 slipped sts over

Inspired by the bold and voluptuous floral patterns of classic English textiles, this seamless design features a large-scale lace motif which encircles the yoke.

Lush and pretty in a vivid red or pink this is a perfect spring cardigan. It is also adorable in tiny sizes, and makes a darling gift for a new baby.

LUSH

materials

Yarn: DK weight yarn: **see table for yardage** (*ladies S sample shown in **Skein Queen Voluptuous** in 'persimmon'*)

Gauge: 20 sts / 4" in stockinette stitch using larger needles

Needles: US #3 / 3.25 mm and US #6 / 4.0 mm; (*or as req'd to meet gauge*) 24"+ circular and double pointed needles in each size

Notions: stitch markers, darning needle, buttons

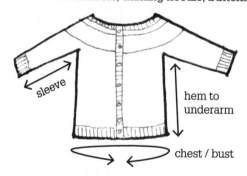

sleeve

hem to underarm

chest / bust

sizing: The pattern includes 8 child and 8 adult sizes:

Size	Chest	Sleeve	Hem to UA	Yardage
0-6 mo	19"	7.5"	6"	280
6-12 mo	20.5"	8"	6.5"	300
1-2 yrs	22"	8.5"	7"	320
2-4 yrs	24"	10.5"	9"	420
5-6 yrs	26"	12"	11"	550
7-8 yrs	27"	14"	13"	650
9-10 yrs	29.5"	16"	14"	750
11-12 yrs	31"	18"	14.5"	850
XS	33"	12"	14.5"	800
S	36"	12.5"	15"	850
M	39"	12.5"	15.5"	950
L	41"	13"	16"	1000
XL	45"	13.5"	16.5"	1100
XXL	50"	13.5"	17"	1250
3XL	55"	14"	17"	1350
4XL	60"	14"	17"	1450

Finished garment measurments given; choose size based on your measurements + desired ease.

sizing notes: Lush is designed to be close-fitting with 1" to 3" negative ease for adult sizes. Nina (38" bust) is wearing S (36") with 2" negative ease. Adult sizes have 3/4 sleeves and optional waist shaping. Child sizes have long sleeves and no body shaping. Waist shaping decreases to 2.5" less than bust size.

Cute as a button! Hunter is wearing the 2-4 yrs size, knit in **Sweet Georgia Superwash DK** in 'silver'.

pattern: First the lace yoke band is knit from centre back outward to left and right. Stitches are picked up along the top edge of the lace yoke band, and the collar is worked. Stitches are picked up along the bottom edge of the band, and worked down yoke to sleeves and hem. Button bands are worked last.

yoke band: Using larger needles, CO 19 (17, 19, 17, 23, 21, 21, 23, **21, 23, 23, 21, 23, 23, 23**) sts **provisionally.** Purl 1 row.

Work RH side of yoke band:

Sizes 0-6 mo to 2-4 years: Starting on row 1 (19, 13, 7) of chart A, work a total of 72 (78, 84, 90) rows following chart (ending with row 24 in each case).

Sizes 5-6 yrs to Adult 4XL: Starting on row - (-, -, -, 1, 25, 25, 17, **9, 1, 17, 9, 1, 17, 1, 17**) of chart B, work a total of - (-, -, -, 96, 104, 104, 112, **120, 128, 144, 152, 160, 176, 192, 208**) rows of chart B (ending with row 32 in each case).

All sizes: Place sts on hold and break yarn.

Unpick provisional cast on and place live sts back on needles. With RS facing, attach yarn and work the LH side of the yoke band same as the RH side. Place sts on hold and break yarn.

You now have a band that forms the yoke of the cardigan. Wet block this band; it should measure approximately 3.25 (4.5) inches wide for chart A (B).

collar: Using larger needles, with RS facing, pick up and knit 72 (78, 84, 90, 96, 104, 104, 112, **120, 128, 144, 152, 160, 176, 192, 208**) sts along the upper edge of the lace yoke band (*approximately one st in every 2 rows*).

Purl 1 row, decreasing 0 (2, 0, 2, 8, 12, 12, 16, **0, 8, 24, 22, 20, 31, 42, 22**) sts, evenly spaced. [72 (76, 84, 88, 88, 92, 92, 96, **120, 120, 120, 130, 140, 145, 150, 186**) sts]

Sizes 0-6 mo to 2-4 years: switch to smaller needles and establish ribbing: k3, (p2, k2) to last stitch, k1. Work 6 more rows as established, then bind off loosely.

Sizes 5-6 years to 11-12 years: Work 2 more rows in stockinette, then switch to smaller needles and establish ribbing: k3, (p2, k2) to last stitch, k1. Work 6 more rows as set, then bind off loosely.

Sizes XS to 4XL: Work 5 more rows in stockinette. Decrease row (WS): [purl 3 (**4, 4, 3, 3, 3, 3, 1**), p2tog] repeat to end. [96 (**100, 100, 104, 112, 116, 120, 124**) sts]

Switch to smaller needles and establish ribbing: k3, (p2, k2) to last stitch, k1
Work 1 more row in ribbing, then work short rows:

Work in pattern to 12 sts before end of row, w&t.
Repeat previous short row once more.
Work in pattern to 8 sts before gap, w&t.
Repeat previous short row 3 more times.

Next 2 rows: work in pattern to end, working wraps together with the sts they wrap.

Work 5 more rows in ribbing then bind off loosely.

key & abbreviations

☐ **k** - knit

☒O **yo** - yarn over

☒ **k2tog** - knit 2 sts together

☒ **ssk** - slip 2 stitches knitwise (one at a time), then knit 2 slipped stitches together through back loops

■ **sl1-k2tog-psso** - slip 1, k2tog, pass slipped st over

▓ **No Stitch** (inserted for clarity of pattern)

chart notes

Charts represent RS rows only; WS rows: purl all sts.
Charts are worked from right to left.
Refer to pattern text for which Row number to start on.

chart A - sizes 0-6 mo to 2-4 yrs

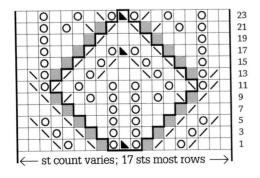

← st count varies; 17 sts most rows →

chart B - sizes 4-5 yrs to adult 4XL

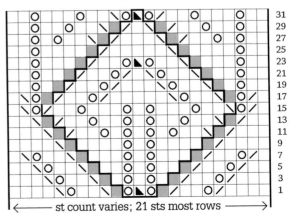

← st count varies; 21 sts most rows →

yoke: Using larger needles, with RS facing, pick up and knit 1 stitch in each row along the lower edge of the yoke band, for a total of 144 (156, 168, 180, 192, 208, 208, 224, **240, 256, 288, 304, 320, 352, 384, 416**) sts. Purl 1 row.

Next row: knit, increasing 8 (8, 0, 0, 8, 0, 12, 4, **0, 8, 4, 0, 8, 0, 8, 12**) sts, evenly spaced. [152 (164, 168, 180, 200, 208, 220, 228, **240, 264, 292, 304, 328, 352, 392, 428**) sts]

Work 1 (3, 5, 7, 3, 5, 5, 7, **7, 7, 9, 9, 9, 11, 13, 13**) rows even, ending with a WS row.

separate arms and body:

Knit 22 (24, 25, 27, 30, 31, 33, 35, **37, 41, 45, 46, 51, 56, 62, 69**) sts (this is L front),

Place next 32 (34, 34, 36, 40, 42, 44, 44, **46, 50, 56, 60, 62, 64, 72, 76**) sts on hold (this is L sleeve),

CO 4 (4, 6, 6, 6, 6, 8, 8, **8, 8, 8, 10, 10, 12, 12, 12**) sts (this is L underarm),

Knit 44 (48, 50, 54, 60, 62, 66, 70, **74, 82, 90, 92, 102, 112, 124, 138**) sts (this is back),

Place sts on hold for R sleeve as at L, CO sts for R underarm as at L, then knit to end.

The sleeve stitches are now on hold, and there are 96 (104, 112, 120, 132, 136, 148, 156, **164, 180, 196, 204, 224, 248, 272, 300**) body sts on the needles.

body: Child sizes are worked straight to ribbed hem. Adult sizes include instructions for optional waist shaping.

body child sizes: work in stockinette until piece measures 4.5 (5, 5.5, 7.5, 9.5, 11.5, 12.5, 13) inches from underarm *(or 1.5" short of desired length).*

Next RS row, switch to smaller needles and establish ribbing: k3, (p2, k2) to last st, k1
Continue in ribbing as established until piece measures 6 (6.5, 7, 9, 11, 13, 14, 14.5) inches from underarm *(or desired length).* Bind off loosely.

body adult sizes: *waist shaping optional*

Work **3.75** (**4, 4, 4.25, 4.25, 4.5, 4.75, 5**) inches in stockinette stitch, then setup for waist shaping.

Setup Row (RS): knit 41 (45, 49, 51, 56, 62, 68, 75) sts, PM, knit 82 (90, 98, 102, 112, 124, 136, 150) sts, PM, knit to end.
Purl 1 row.

Decrease Row: [knit to 4 sts before marker, k2tog, k4, ssk] twice, knit to end.
Work 7 rows even.
Repeat previous 8 rows once more, then work one more decrease row *(12 sts decreased in total).*
[152 (168, 184, 192, 212, 236, 260, 288) sts]

Work 9 rows even.

Increase Row: [knit to 2 sts before marker, m1, k4, m1] twice, knit to end.
Work 7 rows even.
Repeat previous 8 rows once more, then work one

more increase row *(12 sts increased in total).*
[**164** (**180, 196, 204, 224, 248, 272, 300**) sts]

Work in stockinette stitch until piece measures **12.5** (**13, 13.5, 14, 14.5, 15, 15, 15**) inches from underarm, *(or 2 inches short of desired length).*

Next RS row, switch to smaller needles and establish ribbing: k3, (p2, k2) to last st, k1
Continue in ribbing as established until piece measures **14.5** (**15, 15.5, 16, 16.5, 17, 17, 17**) inches from underarm *(or desired length).* Bind off loosely.

sleeves: Place held sts back on larger needles. In stitches CO at underarm, with RS facing, pick up and knit 2 (2, 3, 3, 3, 3, 4, 4, **4, 4, 4, 5, 5, 6, 6, 6**) sts, PM, pick up and knit 2 (2, 3, 3, 3, 3, 4, 4, **4, 4, 4, 5, 5, 6, 6, 6**) sts, knit around held sts, and across the picked-up sts to the marker, which indicates the beginning of round. [36 (38, 40, 42, 46, 48, 52, 52, **54, 58, 64, 70, 72, 76, 84, 88**) sts]

Knit 4 (4, 4, 4, 5, 5, 5, 5, **5, 5, 4, 4, 4, 3, 2.5, 2.5**) inches even from underarm.

Decrease round: k2, ssk, knit to last 4 sts, k2tog, k2
Knit 5 rounds.
Repeat previous 6 rounds until there are 32 (32, 36, 36, 40, 44, 44, 48, **48, 52, 52, 56, 60, 60, 64, 68**) sts.

Work even until sleeve measures 6.5 (7, 7.5, 9.5, 10.75, 12.75, 14.75, 16.75, **10.5, 11, 11, 11.5, 12, 12, 12.5, 12.5**) inches from underarm.

Switch to smaller needles and work 2x2 rib (k2, p2) for 1 (1, 1, 1, 1.25, 1.25, 1.25, 1.25, **1.5, 1.5, 1.5, 1.5, 1.5, 1.5, 1.5, 1.5**) inches. Bind off loosely purlwise and break yarn. Work second sleeve same as first.

button bands: Using smaller needles, with RS facing, pick up and knit approximately 2 sts in every 3 rows. When you get to the held lace band sts, place sts back on needles and knit them, then continue picking up and knitting to the end of the piece. Pick up a multiple of 4 sts. *If you work the non-buttonhole side first, you can use it to plan the number and spacing of buttonholes for the other side.*

Establish Ribbing (WS): p3, (k2, p2) to last stitch, p1
Work 2 more rows in ribbing as established, then work buttonhole row (on one side). Work in pattern, making 5 to 10 buttonholes, evenly spaced in band.

To make a 3-st buttonhole in 1 row: Slip next 2 sts. Pass the first st over the second (bind off), [sl1, bind stitch off] twice. Slip stitch from RH needle to LH needle. Turn work and CO 3 sts knitwise. Turn back and proceed to work to next buttonhole.

If you find this buttonhole is too big or too small, you can work similar buttonholes by binding off then casting on 1, 2, or 4 sts in the same manner.

Work 4-6 more rows in ribbing, then bind off loosely.

finishing: weave in ends, sew buttons to band opposite buttonholes, and block finished garment.

the scottish wild

In contrast to the gentle and lush gardens of the south, Scotland has a wilder nature. Northerly latitudes make for dark and dreary winters and brilliantly long summer days.

Much more compact than the unending wilderness of my native Canada, Scotland's wild places have a different feel and a more subtle, older flavour.

The land has a smoothness: mountains and valleys have been scoured by the passage of time and the movement of glaciers. It also bears marks of inhabitation. The highlanders were a tough breed to survive here with premodern technologies.

Moor, bog, and heather create landscapes of burnt reds and browns which are exquisitely luminous under cloudy skies.

Lochs (lakes) and burns (streams) punctuate the scene, reflecting the sky. Of the north and west coast thousands of islands dot the stormy sea: Skye, the Outer Hebrides, Orkney, and the Shetland Islands among them. These islands have rich histories of wool production that continue today.

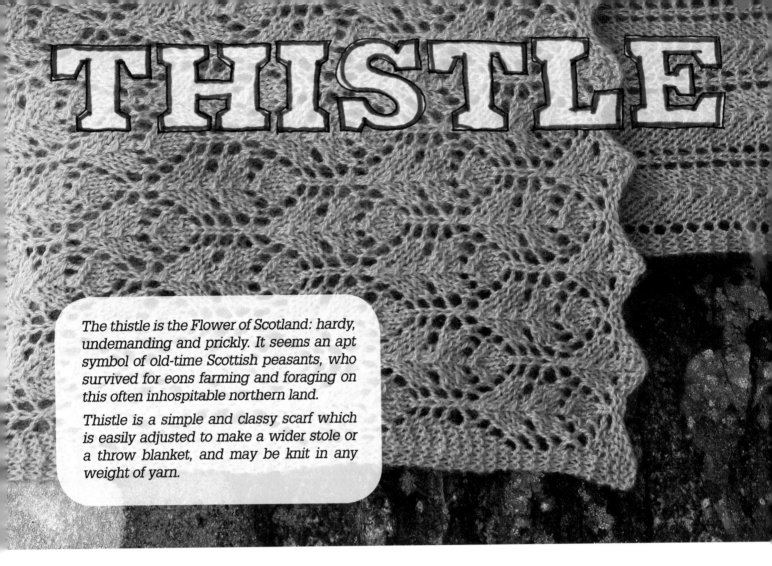

THISTLE

The thistle is the Flower of Scotland: hardy, undemanding and prickly. It seems an apt symbol of old-time Scottish peasants, who survived for eons farming and foraging on this often inhospitable northern land.

Thistle is a simple and classy scarf which is easily adjusted to make a wider stole or a throw blanket, and may be knit in any weight of yarn.

sizing: In 4-ply yarn at suggested gauge, the scarf will measure about 12" wide by 80" long, depending on how aggressively you block the lace. To adjust width, add or subtract a multiple of 10 sts.

materials:

Yarn:	600 yds of sock weight or 4-ply yarn *(sample in **Juno Fibre Arts Belle** in 'golden')*
Needles:	US # 5 / 3.75 mm *(or as req'd to meet gauge)*;
Gauge:	24 sts / 4" in stockinette stitch
Notions:	stitch markers, darning needle

pattern: The scarf is knit in rows from end to end. Cast on 65 stitches loosely. Knit three rows.

thistle lace: Following chart A or written instructions, work rows 1-28 of thistle lace a total of seven times *(or until you have used approximately 1/3 of your yarn or reached 1/3 of desired length)*.

column lace: To transition to the column pattern work rows 1-8 of the thistle lace pattern once more. Then proceed to work transition rows 1-2, (also shown on chart B):

Row 1 (RS): k2, ssk, yo, [k7, yo, s1-k2tog-psso, yo] to last 11 sts, k7, yo, k2tog, k2

Row 2 (WS): k3, purl to last 3 sts, k3

Next work the column pattern rows 3-4 (also shown on chart B:

Row 3 (RS): k3, [yo, k3, s1-k2tog-psso, k3, yo, k1] to last 2 sts, k2

Row 4 (WS): k3, purl to last 3 sts, k3

Repeat rows 3-4 until scarf is desired length, or you are nearly out of yarn. Knit 3 rows, bind off loosely, and wet-block your lace scarf.

chart B: transition & column chart:
work rows 1-2 once, then repeat rows 3-4 to end

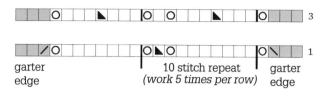

garter edge | 10 stitch repeat *(work 5 times per row)* | garter edge

chart A: thistle lace: repeat rows 1-28

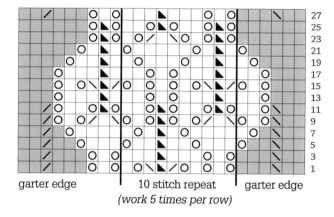

garter edge | 10 stitch repeat *(work 5 times per row)* | garter edge

chart notes

Chart shows RS rows only.
WS rows: knit sts shaded on previous row, purl to last sts, knit sts shaded on previous round *(this creates a garter stitch edge)*.
Charts are read from right to left.

key and abbreviations

☐ **k** - knit

Ⓞ **yo** - yarn over

╱ **k2tog** - knit 2 sts together

╲ **ssk** - slip 2 stitches knitwise (one at a time), then knit 2 slipped stitches together through back loops

◣ **sl1-k2tog-psso** - slip 1, knit 2 together, pass slipped stitch over

▨ shade indicates that stitch is KNIT rather than purled on the following WS row, to create a garter edge.

thistle lace pattern: repeat rows 1-28

Row 1 (RS): k2, ssk, k3, [yo, k1, yo, k1, yo, k2tog, s1-k2tog-psso, ssk, yo, k1] to last 8 sts, yo, k1, yo, k3, k2tog, k2
Rows 2, 4 (WS): k6, purl to last 6 sts, k6
Row 3: k2, ssk, k3, [yo, k1, yo, k3, s1-k2tog-psso, k3] to last 8 sts, yo, k1, yo, k3, k2tog, k2
Row 5: k2, ssk, k2, yo, [k3, yo, k2, s1-k2tog-psso, k2, yo] to last 9 sts, k3, yo, k2, k2tog, k2
Row 6: k5, purl to last 5 sts, k5
Row 7: k2, ssk, k1, yo, k1, [k4, yo, k1, s1-k2tog-psso, k1, yo, k1] to last 9 sts, k4, yo, k1, k2tog, k2
Row 8: k4, purl to last 4 sts, k4
Row 9: k2, ssk, yo, k1, yo, [ssk, k1, k2tog, yo, k1, yo, s1-k2tog-psso, yo, k1, yo] to last 10 sts, ssk, k1, k2tog, yo, k1, yo, k2tog, k2
Rows 10, 12, 14, 16, 18: k3, purl to last 3 sts, k3
Row 11: k2, ssk, yo, k2, [yo, s1-k2tog-psso, yo, k2, yo, s1-k2tog-psso, yo, k2] to last 9 sts, yo, s1-k2tog-psso, yo, k2, yo, k2tog, k2
Row 13: k3, yo, k2, [k1, s1-k2tog-psso, k3, yo, k1, yo, k2] to last 10 sts, k1, s1-k2tog-psso, k3, yo, k3
Row 15: k3, yo, k1, yo, [k2tog, s1-k2tog-psso, ssk, yo, k1, yo, k1, yo], to last 11 sts, k2tog, s1-k2tog-psso, ssk, yo, k1, yo, k3
Row 17: as row 13
Row 19: k4, yo, k1, [k1, s1-k2tog-psso, k2, yo, k3, yo, k1] to last 10 sts, k1, s1-k2tog-psso, k2, yo, k4
Row 20: k4, purl to last 4 sts, k4
Row 21: k5, yo, [k1, s1-k2tog-psso, k1, yo, k5, yo] to last 10 sts, k1, s1-k2tog-psso, k1, yo, k5
Row 22: k5, purl to last 5 sts, k5
Row 23: k6, [yo, s1-k2tog-psso, yo, k1, yo, ssk, k1, k2tog, yo, k1] to last 9 sts, yo, s1-k2tog-psso, yo, k6
Row 24, 26: k6, purl to last 6 sts, k6
Row 25: k6, [yo, s1-k2tog-psso, yo, k2, yo, s1-k2tog-psso, yo, k2] to last 9 sts, yo, s1-k2tog-psso, yo, k6
Row 27: k2, ssk, k3, [yo, k1, yo, k3, s1-k2tog-psso, k3] to last 8 sts, yo, k1, yo, k3, k2tog, k2
Row 28: k6, purl to last 6 sts, k6

An estuary (or 'firth' in Scots) is an in-between place, not ocean, yet no longer river. It is a fertile habitat where sweet and salt water mix, and many species thrive.

Estuary combines two watery lace patterns to create an ambiguous shape: not quite a shawl, yet something more than a scarf.

ESTUARY

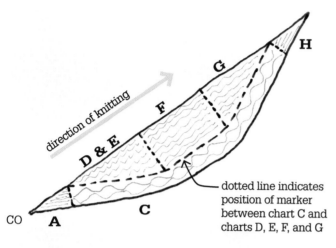

CO · A

direction of knitting

D & E · F · G · H · C

dotted line indicates position of marker between chart C and charts D, E, F, and G

sizing: Finished piece will be approximately 76" long by 16" deep; depending on gauge, yarn, and how aggressively you block the lace.

materials:

Yarn: 600 yds of sock weight or 4-ply yarn *(sample in **Old Maiden Aunt 100% Superwash Merino 4ply** in 'jaded')*

Needles: US #6 / 4.0 mm *(or as req'd to meet gauge)*

Gauge: 24 sts & 32 rows / 4" in stockinette *(correct gauge is not essential for this project, but may affect yardage)*

Notions: stitch markers, darning needle blocking wires (if desired)

pattern: Estuary is knit in rows from end to end. It consists of two different lace patterns set side-by-side as shown in schematic.

beginning: *chart A*

Cast on 2 sts.

Work rows 1-71 of chart A once.   [37 sts]

Setup Row 72 (WS): k2, p3, PM, purl to last 2 sts, k2

Note: This marker will stay in the work throughout, and mark the line between the two lace patterns that form the piece. Continue to slip marker throughout.

Note: Chart B was included in a previously published version of this pattern, but is NOT used in this version.

increase section: *charts C & D, then C & E*

Work row 1 of chart C to marker, slip marker, work row 1 of chart D to end.

Continue, working rows 2-20 of charts C and D once. [43 sts]

Begin working chart E in place of chart D:
Work row 21 of chart C to marker, slip marker, work row 1 of chart E to end.

Continue working charts as established, repeating rows 1-40 of chart C and rows 1-20 of chart E, until five total repeats of chart E have been worked, ending on row 40 of chart C.

[78 sts; 32 sts to the right of the marker and 46 sts to the left of the marker (with RS facing)]

If at this point you wish to widen the shawl, you can work further repeats of charts C and E, always ending on row 40 of chart C.

even section: *charts C & F*

Work row 1 of chart C to marker, slip marker, work row 1 of chart F to end.

Continue working charts as established, repeating rows 1-40 of chart C and rows 1-20 of chart F until four total repeats of chart F have been worked, ending on row 40 of chart C.

If at this point you wish to lengthen the shawl, you can work further repeats of charts C and F, always ending on row 40 of chart C.

decrease section: *charts C & G, then H*

Work row 1 of chart C to marker, slip marker, work row 1 of chart G to end.

Continue working charts as established, work rows 2-20 of chart G once.

[73 sts; 32 sts to the right of marker and 41 sts to the left of the marker (with RS facing)]

Continue as established, working rows 21-40 of chart G a total of four times, then finally work rows 41-60 of chart G once, ending on row 40 of chart C.

Note: if you worked extra repeats of chart E, you will need to work rows 21-40 of chart G more times to correspond, until 13 sts remain to the left of marker, then proceed to work rows 41-60 of chart G.

[38 sts; 32 sts to the right of marker and 6 sts to the left of the marker (with RS facing)]

Work rows 1-72 of chart H across all sts, removing the marker. Bind off remaining 2 sts.

finishing: Weave in ends and wet-block shawl.

chart A - work rows 1-71 once. See text for row 72 (Setup).

chart H - work rows 1-72

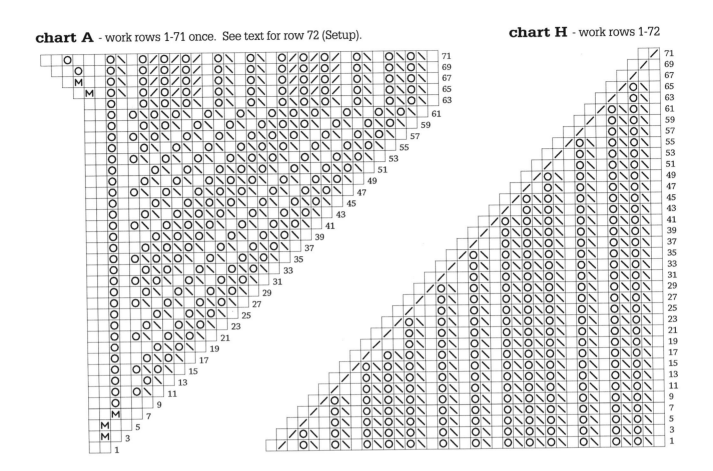

chart E - work rows 1-20 five times

second repeat of chart E shown for clarity only

edge sts   7 st repeat   edge sts

chart C - repeat rows 1-40

Dotted line indicates marker placement between chart C and charts D, E, F, and G

edge st

← 13 st repeat → worked twice

edge sts

chart D - work rows 1-20 once

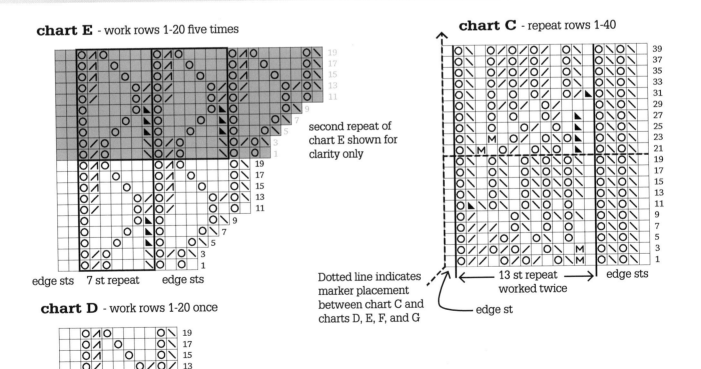

increase section charts

chart notes

Charts represent RS rows only - WS rows: k2, purl to last 2 sts, k2

Charts are read from right to left.

Refer to pattern text and schematic for the order of charts, number of chart repeats, stitch counts, and how to adjust finished size by working more or less repeats.

Chart C is shown alongside charts E, F, G for clarity during knitting, but it is identical in each place. Chart B is not required in this version (it was used in a previously published version of pattern).

Where segments of charts are shaded, this indicates additional repeats of pattern or chart shown for clarity.

key & abbreviations

- ☐ **k** - knit
- Ⓞ **yo** - yarn over
- Ⓜ **m1** - make 1 stitch
- ╱ **k2tog** - knit 2 together
- ╲ **ssk** - slip 2 stitches knitwise (one at a time), then knit 2 slipped stitches together through back loops
- ⟋ **k3tog** - knit 3 sts together
- ◣ **sl1-k2tog-psso** - slip 1 st, k2tog, pass slipped stitch over
- ⋀ **sl2-k2tog-p2sso** - slip 2 sts, k2tog, pass 2 slipped stitches over

decrease section charts

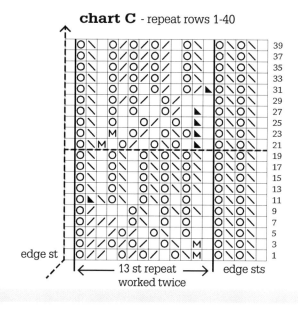

chart C - repeat rows 1-40

edge st ← 13 st repeat → edge sts
worked twice

chart G -
work rows 1-20 once
work rows 21-40 four times
work rows 41-60 once

edge sts   7 st repeat   7 st repeat   edge sts

even section charts

second repeat of chart F shown for clarity only

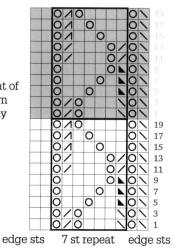

chart F - work rows 1-20 four times

edge sts   7 st repeat   edge sts

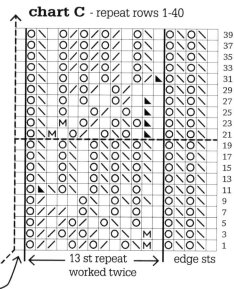

chart C - repeat rows 1-40

edge st ← 13 st repeat → edge sts
worked twice

LOCH

Loch is inspired by the pristine reflections and rippling waters of Scotland. The organic lace pattern that adorns the hat and mittens is reminiscent of flukes, fish tails, and flowing water.

Cute on the kiddies! Hunter is wearing the toddler size, knit in Gourmet Crafter Cashmere in 'stay golden'.

sizing:

Hat: baby (toddler, child, adult S/M, L)
Fits head: 16 (18, 20, 22, 24)" around
samples shown are adult S/M and toddler sizes

Mittens: toddler (child, adult S/M, adult L)
Hand circumference: 6 (7, 7.75, 8.5) inches
Finished length: 9 (9.5, 11, 11.5) inches

materials:

Yarn: Sport weight yarn
Hat: 100 (120, 150, 175, 220) yds
Mittens: 110 (150, 220, 240) yds
*(samples shown in **Skein Queen Opulent 100% Cashmere** in 'cloudless')*

Gauge: 26 sts / 4" in stockinette on smaller needles

Needles: US #2 / 2.75 mm and US #3 / 3.25mm;
or as req'd to meet gauge; 16 inch circular and double pointed needles in each size

Notions: stitch markers, darning needle

6 (7, 7.5, 8, 9)"

16 (18, 20, 22, 24)"

9 (9.5, 11, 11.5)"

6 (7, 7.75, 8.5)"

Eilean Donan Castle - Loch Duich, Scotland

hat pattern: Using smaller needles CO 80 (90, 88, 110, 120) sts, PM, and join for working in the round.

Setup round: [(p1, k1) 8 (9, 11, 11, 12) times, PM] around

Markers now separate the work into 5 (5, 4, 5, 5) sections each with 16 (18, 22, 22, 24) sts.

Work in ribbing as set for 9 (11, 13, 13, 11) more rounds. Switch to larger needles.

Increase Round:
Baby: [p1, k5, p1, k1, m1, k1, m1, k1, p1, k5] around
Toddler: [p1, k1, p1, k5, p1, k1, m1, k1, m1, k1, p1, k5] around
Child and Adult S/M): [p1, (k2, m1) twice, (k1, p1) 6 times, k1, (m1, k2) twice] around
Adult L: [p1, (k1, p1) 4 times, m1, k1, m1, k7, m1, k1, m1, (p1, k1) 3 times] around [90 (100, 104, 130, 140) sts]

Establish lace pattern -
Baby: [p1, work chart A] around
Toddler: [p1, k1, p1, work chart A] around
Child and Adult S/M): [p1, work chart B] around
Adult L: [p1, k1, p1, work chart B] around.
For adult L only you will start chart B on round 13.

All even number rounds: work in pattern, knitting the knits and yarn-overs, and purling the purls.

Baby (Toddler): Work rounds 1-16 of chart A 1 (2) times, then work rounds 1-8 once more.
Child (Adult S/M): Work rounds 1-24 of chart B once, then work rounds 1-12 once more.
Adult L: Work rounds 13-24 of chart B once, work rounds 1-24 once, then work rounds 1-12 once more.

This is a total of 24 (40, 36, 36, 48) rounds.

decreases: *switch to dpns when necessary.*

Baby: [p1, work chart C] around
Toddler: [p1, k1, p1, work chart C] around
Child and Adult S/M): [p1, work chart E] around
Adult L: [p1, k1, p1, work chart E] around

Work to end of round 15 (15, 23, 23, 23) of chart C (C, E, E, E). [10 (20, 8, 10, 20) sts]

Next Round: ssk around [5 (10, 4, 5, 10) sts]

Break yarn, thread tail through remaining sts and pull tight to close top of hat.

finishing: Weave in all ends and wet-block hat. For a slouchy fit, block the lace aggressively over a plate, or for a snug fit simply pat into shape.

key & abbreviations

☐ **k** - knit

• **p** - purl

Ⓞ **yo** - yarn over

⟋ **k2tog** - knit 2 together

⟍ **ssk** - slip 2 stitches knitwise (one at a time), then knit 2 slipped stitches together through back loops

⋀ **sl2-k1-psso** - slip 2 stitches together, k1, pass 2 slipped sts over

chart notes

Refer to pattern text for which charts to use, and which row number to start on for your size.

Charts represent odd number rounds only.
Even number rounds: continue in pattern as established (knit the knits and yo's and purl the purls)

Charts are read from right to left.

chart F - adult mittens

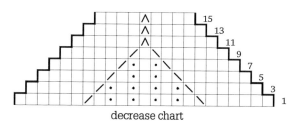

decrease chart

chart D - toddler and child mittens

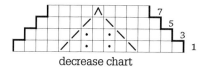

decrease chart

chart E -
child, adult S/M and L beanie

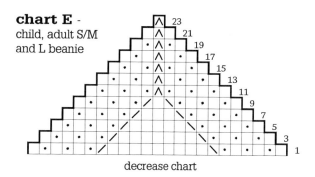

decrease chart

chart C - baby and toddler beanie

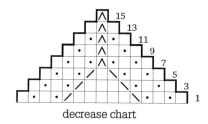

decrease chart

chart B - child, adult S/M and L beanie and adult mittens

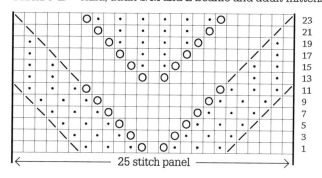

chart A - baby and toddler beanie and toddler and child mittens

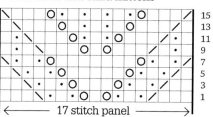

mitten pattern: Mittens are knit in the round from cuff to fingertips.

cuff: Using smaller needles CO 38 (42, 54, 58) sts, PM, and join for working in the round.

Setup Ribbing:
Toddler (Child): [p1(2), (k1, p1) 9 times, p0(1)] twice
Adult S/M (L): [p1(2), (k1, p1) 13 times, p0(1)] twice

Work 15 (19, 15, 19) more rounds in ribbing as established.

Lace pattern is worked on palm and back of mittens.

Establish lace pattern:
Toddler (Child): [p1(2), work chart A, p1(2)] twice
Adult S/M (L): [p1(2), work chart B, p1(2)] twice

Work in pattern as established until you have completed a total of 16 (8, 24, 14) chart rounds. On the next round: chart A (A, B, B) round 1 (9, 1, 15), begin the thumb gusset, while continuing lace pattern at back of hand and palm as established.

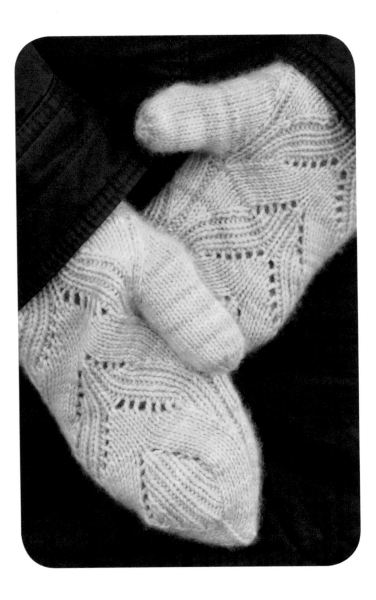

thumb gusset: the thumb gusset is worked at the beginning of the round. Left and right hand mittens are worked the same.

Round 1: m1, PM, work in pattern to end.
There is now 1 stitch in the thumb gusset section between BOR marker and new marker.
Rounds 2 & 4: knit to marker, work in pattern to end
Round 3: m1, k1, m1, slip marker, work as set to end
Round 5: k1, m1, knit to 1 st before marker, m1, k1, work in pattern to end
Round 6: knit to marker, work in pattern to end
Repeat rounds 5-6 until there are 13 (15, 17, 19) sts in the thumb gusset section between the first 2 markers.
[51 (57, 71, 77) sts]

Next round: Place the 13 (15, 17, 19) thumb gusset sts on hold. Work to end of round as established.
[38 (42, 54, 58) sts]

hand: continue in lace pattern (as at cuff) until you have worked 3 repeats of chart A (A, B, B) in total *(this is 48 (48, 72, 72) chart rounds)*.

decreases: *switch to dpns when necessary.*
Toddler (Child): [p1(2), work chart D, p1(2)] twice
Adult S/M (L): [p1(2), work chart F, p1(2)] twice

Work to end of round 7 (7, 15, 15) of chart E (E, F, F).

Rnd 1: [p1(2, 1, 2), k3, sl2-k1-p2sso, k3, p1(2, 1, 2)] twice
Rnd 2: [p1(2, 1, 2), k2, sl2-k1-p2sso, k2, p1(2, 1, 2)] twice
Rnd 3: p1(2, 1, 2), k1, sl2-k1-p2sso, k1, p1(2, 1, 2) twice
Rnd 4: p1(2, 1, 2), sl2-k1-p2sso, p1(2, 1, 2) twice
[6 (10, 6, 10) sts]

Break yarn, thread tail through remaining sts, and pull tight to close top of mitten.

thumb: Place 13 (15, 17, 19) held sts back on needles. Attach yarn and pick up and knit 3 sts in mitten body, then knit around held sts.
[16 (18, 20, 22) sts]

PM and join for working in the round. Knit in rounds until thumb measures 1.25 (1.5, 2.0, 2.25) inches *(or just short of total desired length)*.

Next round: k2tog around [8 (9, 10, 11) sts]
Next round: k2tog to last 0 (1, 0, 1) sts, k0 (1, 0, 1)

Break yarn, thread tail through remaining 4 (5, 5, 6) sts, and pull tight to close top of thumb.

finishing: Weave in all ends and block mittens.

WIND

Isle of Skye, Scotland

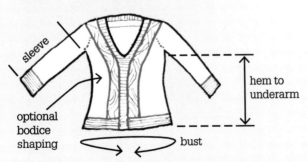

Bright and cheery! Hunter is wearing the 1-2 yr size, knit in **Morgan's Fine Yarns Glamorgan** in 'goldenrod'.

materials:

Yarn: DK weight yarn: **see table for yardage** (*sample shown in **Shilasdair Luxury DK with Camel** in 'fleece cloud'*)

Gauge: 22 sts & 26 rows / 4" in stockinette stitch

Needles: US #6 / 4.0 mm (*or as req'd to meet gauge*) circular and double pointed needles

Notions: stitch markers, darning needle

sleeve

optional bodice shaping

bust

hem to underarm

sizing: pattern includes 8 child and 8 adult sizes:

Size	Chest	Sleeve	Hem to UA	Yardage
0-6 mo	19"	7.5"	7"	375
6-12 mo	20.5"	8"	8"	400
1-2 yrs	22"	8.5"	9"	450
2-4 yrs	24"	10"	10"	500
5-6 yrs	25"	13"	11"	600
7-8 yrs	26"	15"	13"	700
9-10 yrs	27"	16"	14"	800
11-12 yrs	28"	17"	15"	900
XS	28"	18"	16"	950
S	32"	19"	17"	1000
M	34.5"	20"	17"	1100
L	37"	20"	18"	1200
XL	42"	20"	18"	1300
XXL	46"	21"	18"	1400
3XL	51"	21"	18"	1500
4XL	56"	21"	18"	1600

Finished garment measurements given; choose size based on your measurements + desired ease.

sizing notes :

Adults, choose a size 1-3 inches smaller than your bust measurement, this fitted pullover should cling over bust. Nina (38" bust) is wearing size M (34.5").

SWEPT

The north and west coasts of Scotland are dotted with islands, many little more than rocks strewn in a cold and stormy sea. These are windswept places: landscapes scoured round and smooth by time, glaciers, and ocean winds.

This pullover features a lace panel inspired by this wave-battered landscape, knit in a yarn dyed on the Isle of Skye.

pattern: Windswept is knit seamlessly from the top down. First the lace collar band is knit from centre back outward to right and left. Stitches are picked up along the edge of this band, and the yoke is worked in rows. Sleeve stitches are placed on hold, and the body is worked first in rows, then joined for working in the round to hem. Sleeves are knit last.

collar: Cast on 17 (17, 17, 17, 17, 19, 19, 19, **22, 22, 24, 24, 24, 24, 24, 24**) sts **provisionally**.

First WS row: k4 (4, 4, 4, 4, 6, 6, 6, **6, 6, 8, 8, 8, 8, 8, 8**), purl to last 3 sts, k3

garter & lace panel: once established, the garter & lace panels continue as set throughout collar, yoke, and body. '**Work panel**' means continue working the garter & lace panel as established.

right side of collar: Using the R panel chart for your size, work a total of 30 (32, 34, 34, 34, 36, 36, 38, **42, 44, 44, 52, 56, 62, 66, 72**) rows of chart, ending with a WS row. Place sts on hold and break yarn.

left side of collar: Unpick provisional cast on and place sts back on needles. With RS facing, attach yarn and work a total of 30 (32, 34, 34, 34, 36, 36, 38, **42, 44, 44, 52, 56, 62, 66, 72**) rows following the L panel chart for your size. Do not break yarn. You now have a band that forms the collar of the garment.

yoke: To begin the yoke you will work panels and pick up stitches along the edge of the collar.

Pickup Row (RS): Work L panel as set, PM, turn work 90 degrees, then pick up and knit 60 (64, 66, 68, 68, 72, 72, 74, **84, 88, 88, 104, 112, 124, 132, 144**), evenly spaced, along edge of collar (*approximately 1 stitch in every row*), PM, then work R panel.

WS row: work WS of panels, purl all other sts [94 (98, 100, 102, 102, 110, 110, 112, **128, 132, 136, 152, 160, 172, 180, 192**) sts]

Increase Row (RS): work panel, slip marker, (k2, m1) to marker, work panel. [124 (130, 133, 136, 136, 146, 146, 149, **170, 176, 180, 204, 216, 234, 246, 264**) sts]

Setup row (WS): work panel, slip marker, p1, m1p, PM, p25 (26, 26, 26, 26, 28, 28, 29, **35, 35, 34, 43, 45, 49, 51, 55**) sts, PM, p38 (42, 45, 48 ,48, 50, 50, 51, **54, 60, 62, 68, 76, 86, 94, 104**) sts, PM, p25 (26, 26, 26, 26, 28, 28, 29, **35, 35, 34, 43, 45, 49, 51, 55**) sts, PM, m1p, p1, slip marker, work panel. [126 (132, 135, 138, 138, 148, 148, 151, **172, 178, 182, 206, 218, 236, 248, 266**) sts]

The markers separate the work into 7 sections; L panel, L front, L sleeve, back, R sleeve, R front, R panel. Raglan increases will occur at the divisions between fronts, sleeves, and back panels.

raglan increases: follow instructions for your size

Sizes 0-6 months to Adult L:
Row 1 (RS): work panel, slip marker, [knit 1 st before next marker, m1, k2, m1] four times, knit to panel, work panel (8 sts inc)
Row 2 (WS): work WS of panels, purl all other sts
Work rows 1-2 a total of 4 (4, 5, 6, 7, 8, 8, 9, **8, 9, 11, 12, -, -, -, -**) times. [158 (164, 175, 186, 194, 212, 212, 223, **236, 250, 270, 302, -, -, -, -**) sts]

Sizes XL (XXL, 3XL, 4XL):
Work rows 1-2 (as described above) a total of **9 (5, 3, 2**) times. [**290 (276, 272, 282**) sts]

Row 3 (RS): work panel, k2, m1, [knit 1 st before next marker, m1, k2, m1] four times, knit to 2 sts before panel, m1, k2, work panel (10 sts inc)
Row 4 (WS): work WS of panel, purl all other sts
Work rows 3-4 a total of **4 (9, 13, 16**) times. [**330 (366, 402, 442**) sts]

All Sizes: work 2 (2, 2, 2, 2, 2, 2, **4, 4, 4, 2, 0, 0, 0, 0**) more rows without increasing, ending with a WS row.

Child Size Charts

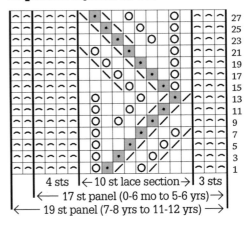

L panel rep rows 1-28

purl on RS, knit on WS row following

3 sts | ← 10 st lace section → | 4 sts
← 17 st panel (0-6 mo to 5-6 yrs) →
← 19 st panel (7-8 yrs to 11-12 yrs) →

R panel repeat rows 1-28

4 sts | ← 10 st lace section → | 3 sts
← 17 st panel (0-6 mo to 5-6 yrs) →
← 19 st panel (7-8 yrs to 11-12 yrs) →

key & abbreviations

☐ **k** - knit

▣ **p** - purl (knit on following WS row)

⊙ **yo** - yarn over

╱ **k2tog** - knit 2 sts together

╲ **ssk** - slip 2 stitches knitwise (one at a time), then knit 2 slipped stitches together through back loops

⌒ **garter stitch** - knit on RS, knit on following WS row. When knit in rounds, knit on odd number round, then purl on following even number round.

chart notes

Charts represent RS rows (odd number rounds) only.

WS rows: Knit the garter edge sts. Knit the sts worked as purls on the previous round (shaded sts), purl all other sts.
Even number Rounds: Purl the garter edge sts. Purl the sts worked as purls on the previous row (shaded sts), knit all other sts.

Read charts from right to left.

Adduct Size Charts

L panel repeat rows 1-40 — purl on RS, knit on WS row following

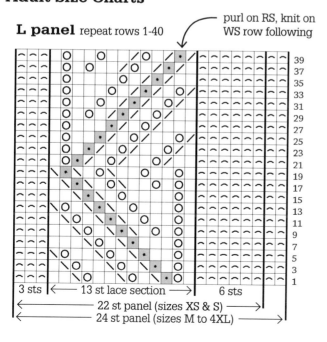

3 sts | 13 st lace section | 6 sts
22 st panel (sizes XS & S)
24 st panel (sizes M to 4XL)

R panel repeat rows 1-40 — garter edge sts: knit on RS, and knit on WS

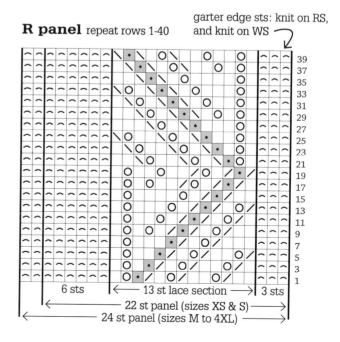

6 sts | 13 st lace section | 3 sts
22 st panel (sizes XS & S)
24 st panel (sizes M to 4XL)

separate arms and body: on a RS row:

Work panel, knit 6 (6, 7, 8, 9, 10, 10, 11, **10, 11, 13, 14, 19, 25, 31, 36**) sts *(L front)*,

Place next 33 (34, 36, 38, 40, 44, 44, 47, **51, 53, 56, 67, 71, 77, 83, 91**) sts on hold *(L sleeve)*,

CO 6 (6, 6, 6, 6, 6, 8, 8, **8, 10, 10, 10, 12, 12, 14, 14**) sts *(L underarm)*,

Knit 46 (50, 55, 60, 62, 66, 66, 69, **70, 78, 84, 92, 102, 114, 126, 140**) sts *(this is back)*,

Place sts on hold for R sleeve as at L, CO sts for R underarm as at L, then work in pattern to end.

The sleeve sts are on hold and there are 104 (108, 115, 122, 126, 136, 140, 145, **150, 164, 178, 188, 212, 236, 264, 288**) body sts on needles.

Work 3 (1, 1, 1, 1, 1, 1, 1, **5, 3, 5, 3, 1, 1, 1, 1**) rows even in pattern (ending with a WS row).

v-neck shaping: Continue working in rows, increasing alongside the panel on each side.

Row 1 (RS): work panel, k2, m1, knit to 2 sts before panel, m1, k2, work panel   [2 sts inc'd]
Row 2:   work WS of panel, purl all other sts
Work rows 1-2 a total of 2 (4, 5, 7, 7, 7, 7, 7, **6, 9, 9, 12, 12, 12, 12, 13**) times. [108 (116, 125, 136, 140, 150, 154, 159, **162, 182, 196, 212, 236, 260, 288, 314**) sts]

join: Next row (RS): work in pattern to last 4 (4, 4, 4, 4, 6, 6, 6, **6, 6, 8, 8, 8, 8, 8, 8**) garter edge sts. Place these final sts on a separate needle, and hold them in front of the first stitches of the row. Knit the last sts together, one for one, with the garter edge sts at the other side, thus creating the overlapped v-neck join. Place marker to indicate the new beginning of round which is located at the start of the lace section of the L panel. From this point forward, omit the first 4 (4, 4, 4, 4, 6, 6, 6, **6, 6, 8, 8, 8, 8, 8, 8**) sts of the L chart. [104 (112, 121, 132, 136, 144, 148, 153, **156, 176, 188, 204, 228, 252, 280, 306**) body sts]

Note: if you continue in rows as set rather than joining in the round, you can easily make a cardigan rather than a pullover; with a shawl-pin for a closure or buttonholes worked at regular intervals in the garter-stitch band.

body adult sizes: Work bodice shaping as described, or simply work in rounds to garter hem.

Work 8 (**10, 12, 8, 10, 10, 10, 10**) rounds in pattern. *You may work further rounds at this point if necessary for work to extend just past widest point of bust.*

Round 1 (dec): work L panel, k1, ssk, knit to 3 sts before R panel, k2tog, k1, work panel to end.
Round 2: work as established
Work rounds 1-2 a total of **4 (5, 6, 6, 7, 7, 8, 8**) times [148 (**166, 176, 192, 214, 238, 264, 290**) sts]. *(You may decrease more or less here, as suits your curves).*

Rounds 3, 4, 5, 6, 7, 8:   work as established
Round 9 (inc): work L panel, k2, m1, knit to 2 sts before R panel, m1, k2, work R panel to end.
Work rounds 3-9 a total of **4 (5, 6, 6, 7, 7, 8, 8**) times [156 (**176, 188, 204, 228, 252, 280, 306**) sts]. *(You may increase more or less here, as suits your hips).*

Work in pattern as set until work measures **14 (15, 15, 16, 16, 16, 16, 16**) inches from underarm *(or 2 inches short of total desired length).*

Setup round: (p4, p2tog) to last **0 (2, 2, 0, 0, 0, 4, 0**) sts, purl to end. [130 (**147, 157, 170, 190, 210, 234, 255**) sts]

Work in garter stitch (knit 1 round, purl 1 round) for 2 inches. Bind off all stitches loosely.

body childrens sizes: After join, childrens sizes are simply worked in the round to the hem. Work in pattern as set until work measures 6 (7, 8, 9, 10, 12, 13, 14) inches from underarm *(or 1 inch short of desired length).*

Setup round: (p4, p2tog) to last 2 (4, 1, 0, 4, 0, 4, 3) sts, purl to end. [87 (94, 101, 110, 114, 120, 124, 128) sts]

Work in garter stitch (knit 1 round, purl 1 round) for 1 inch, then bind off loosely.

sleeves: Work both sleeves the same.

Place held sts back on needles. In the stitches CO at underarm, with RS facing, pick up and knit 3 (3, 3, 3, 3, 3, 4, 4, **4, 5, 5, 5, 6, 6, 7, 7**) sts, PM, pick up and knit 3 (3, 3, 3, 3, 3, 4, 4, **4, 5, 5, 5, 6, 6, 7, 7**) sts, knit around held sts, and across the picked-up sts to the marker, which indicates the beginning of round. [39 (40, 42, 44, 46, 50, 52, 55, **59, 63, 66, 77, 83, 89, 97, 105**) sts]

Knit 2 (2, 3, 4, 7, 7, 7, 7, **8, 8, 9, 5, 6, 6, 4, 3**) inches even from underarm.

Decrease round: k1, ssk, knit to last 3 sts, k2tog, k1
Knit 6 (6, 6, 6, 6, 6, 6, 6, **6, 6, 5, 5, 4, 4, 4, 4**) rounds. Work decrease round again.

Repeat previous 7 (7, 7, 7, 7, 7, 7, 7, **7, 7, 6, 6, 5, 5, 5, 5**) rounds until there are 33 (34, 36, 38, 40, 40, 42, 43, **49, 51, 52, 55, 57, 61, 65, 67**) sts.

Knit until sleeve measures 6.5 (7, 7.5, 9, 12, 14, 15, 16, **16, 17, 18, 18, 18, 19, 19, 19**) inches from underarm.

Setup round: (p4, p2tog) to last 3 (4, 0, 2, 4, 4, 0, 1, **1, 3, 4, 1, 3, 1, 5, 1**) sts, purl to end. [28 (29, 30, 32, 34, 34, 35, 36, **41, 43, 44, 46, 48, 51, 55, 56**) sts]

Work in garter stitch (knit 1 round, purl 1 round) for 1 (**2**) inches for child (**adult**) sizes. Bind off loosely.

finishing: weave in all ends and block finished garment to relax the fabric, smooth out the increase sections, and open up the lace pattern.

happy endings

Since my arrival in this fairy-tale city I have worked hard to create a life for myself here. There have been many late nights; some filled with last minute knitting, and others with comedy shows and ceilidhs.

I rented a room, got a part-time job, and Alexa and I worked our asses off to make Tin Can Knits a reality. Somewhere along the way, I met an adorable Scot and fell in love.

John and I now wear rings on our fingers, and curse our naughty kitten Willow as she cavorts around the house and attacks my yarn. Tin Can Knits Edinburgh studio has a great view to Arthur's Seat, and I am fortunate to work full time designing exquisite patterns for your knitting pleasure!

Edinburgh is chilly, and I miss summer swimming, but it is sweater weather most days - what better climate for a knit designer?

This happy ending is really only a beginning. I have many more adventures in front of me: travel, new designs, and new experiences. Business, man, kitten, ring... What will come next?

What I create tends to be a reflection of my desire. This collection of lace designs reflects a desire for a complex, feminine beauty. The last design in the book illustrates my not-so-secret desire to start a family... Perhaps there will be more baby patterns coming soon!

SPARKLE.

VIVID

Most of my life I have been ambivalent about babies. I was quite surprised that turning 30 and meeting a handsome man who wants kids has changed my outlook...

Now I'm having vivid daydreams about a future that includes little ones, and these fantasies have begun to materialize in knitting!

Vivid is lace patchwork that can be knit in any weight of yarn. I made a baby blanket size in a range of bright primaries.

sizing: The pattern can be knit in any weight of yarn, and you may make more or less squares for a smaller or larger finished blanket.

Squares will measure approximately 7.5 (9, 10.5) inches square for sock (DK, aran) weight yarns.

The baby-blanket sized sample is made in sock weight yarn and is 30 x 37.5 inches (20 squares).

materials: *Yarn amounts given are for 1 square*

sock or 4-ply:	70 yds per square
DK weight:	100 yds per square
worsted / aran:	130 yds per square

*(baby blanket shown in **Jamieson & Smith Jumper Weight**, 20 squares, weighs 225 g, in colours: 23, 91, 121, 125, 93, 1403, 9113, 1280, 75, FC34, 132, FC41, 142)*

Gauge: I recommend that you knit a square using suggested needles, block it and see if you like the finished size and density.

Suggested needles:

sock or 4-ply:	US # 5 / 3.75 mm
DK weight:	US # 7 / 4.5 mm
worsted / aran:	US # 9 / 5.5 mm

Notions: stitch markers, darning needle

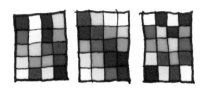

Possible blanket configurations: stripes, blend, or patchwork - play with yours and see what you prefer!

pattern: Vivid is knit one square at a time, then seamed together at the end. Each square is knit from the centre outward to the garter stitch border. Blocking is essential for a beautiful finished result.

square: Using **pinhole method**, cast on 8 sts. Work in the round following charts or text instructions.

vivid lace pattern: work rounds 1-19 following charts or written pattern.

Round 1:	[k1, yo] around [16 sts]	
Round 2 and following even number rounds: knit		
Round 3:	[k2, yo] around	[24 sts]
Round 5:	[k3, yo] around	[32 sts]
Round 7:	[k4, yo] around	[40 sts]
Round 9:	[k2, k2tog, yo, k1, yo] around	[48 sts]
Round 11:	[k1, k2tog, yo, k3, yo] around	[56 sts]
Round 13:	[k2tog, yo, k5, yo] around	[64 sts]

After round 14, proceed to round 15, taking note of the fact that the pattern repeat is now worked 4 times each round.

Round 15: [k1, yo, k1, yo, ssk, k4, yo, k1, yo, k4, k2tog, yo, k1, yo] around [80 sts]

Round 17: [k1, (yo, k3, yo, ssk, k1, k2tog) twice, yo, k3, yo] around [88 sts]

Round 19: [k1, (yo, k5, yo, sl1-k2tog-psso) twice, yo, k5, yo] around [96 sts]

Round 20 (Setup): [k24, PM] around

After working rounds 1-20, you may continue working the square in the same colour, or switch to work the garter stitch border in a contrast colour.

Round 1: [k1, kf&b, knit to 1 sts before marker, kf&b] around
Round 2: [k1, purl to marker] around

Repeat Rounds 1-2 four more times. [136 sts]
Bind off all stitches loosely. Block the first square to determine whether the bind-off method you have chosen is stretchy enough, and that the density / gauge is pleasing to you.

finishing: Wet-block all squares to the same dimensions, arrange into a pleasing composition, then sew the squares together using your preferred method. I butted the edges of squares together (RS facing) and used an overhand seam, catching loops from the bind-off on each side.

vivid lace square - work rounds 1-19

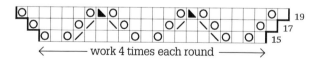

← work 4 times each round →

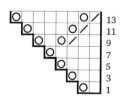

13
11
9
7
5
3
1

work 8 times each round

key & abbreviations

☐ **k** - knit

Ⓞ **yo** - yarn over

⟋ **k2tog** - knit 2 together

⟍ **ssk** - slip 2 stitches knitwise (one at a time), then knit 2 slipped stitches together through back loops

◣ **sl1-k2tog-psso** - slip 1, k2tog, pass slipped st over

chart notes

Charts represent odd numbered rounds only. Even numbered rounds: knit all sts. Charts are worked from right to left.

abbrev.

BOR	beginning of round (marker)
CO	cast on
dec	decrease(d)
dpns	double pointed needles
inc	increas(ed)
k	knit
k2tog	knit 2 stitches together
k3tog	knit 3 stitches together
kf&b	knit into the front and back of one stitch
k-tbl	knit through the back loop of stitch
L(H)	left (hand)
m1	make one knit stitch (any method)
m1p	make one purl stitch (using LH needle, lift bar between sts, and purl through front loop
p	purl
p2tog	purl 2 stitches together
p3tog	purl 3 stitches together
PM	place maker
rep	repeat
RS	right side of the work (public side)
R(H)	right (hand)
sl1	slip one stitch (purlwise unless stated)
sl1-k2tog-psso	slip 1 knitwise, knit 2 together, pass slipped stitch over
sl2-k1-p2sso	slip 2 stitches knitwise at once, knit 1 stitch, pass slipped stitches over
ssk	slip 2 stitches knitwise (one at a time), then knit 2 slipped stitches together through back loops
st. st.	stockinette stitch
st(s)	stitch(es)
tbl	through back loop(s) of stitch(es)
yds	yards
yo	yarn over (yarn forward / yfwd)
WS	wrong side of the work (private side)
w&t	short row wrap & turn
work as established or 'as set' or 'in pattern'	continue in pattern; knit the knit stitches and purl the purls from the previous row. In lace, you typically knit the yo sts (or purl on the WS) and purl the p2togs (or knit on the WS)

This book is intended as a pattern collection, not a technical reference. Some of the advanced techniques used in our patterns are briefly described here.

For step-by-step tutorials covering these techniques in greater depth, visit **www.tincanknits.com**.

blocking: Blocking consists of washing your knit and letting it dry so the stitches relax into their final form. Blocking radically improves most knitted projects. For lace projects it is crucial. To wet block lace, allow piece to soak until saturated, squeeze out as much water as possible in a towel, then pull it tightly and pin it into place. Leave until completely dry, then unpin and admire your work!

casting on and binding off: There are many methods for casting on and binding off. To achieve an excellent finished result you must pay attention at cast on and bind off points. If the first method you try doesn't look right, try another or use different needles to alter your tension.

charts: Chart are read from right to left, and from bottom (row 1) to top. Each square represents a stitch (as indicated by the key). Repeats are indicated by heavy lines, and are worked as many times as will fit in each row. While some charts illustrate every row, others illustrate only RS or odd numbered rows, with the WS or even numbered rows described by text instructions, and/or in the chart notes. Always read chart notes and key carefully before you begin.

picking up stitches: With RS facing, insert needle between sts (or rows), yarn over with working yarn on WS, and pull a loop through knitted fabric to RS (*one st picked up*). Repeat until desired sts have been picked up (*this technique is also referred to as 'pick up and knit' in some patterns*).

pinhole cast on: Used to start a piece of knitting from the centre out, this technique is fiddly the first few times, but becomes easier with practice. To begin, create a circle using the end of the yarn. Hold the circle in your LH, and the needle and working yarn in your RH. You create new sts using the point of the needle, working into the centre of the circle.

1. Insert needle into circle from front to back
2. Wrap yarn around needle (at back)
3. Use needle point to bring loop through circle from back to front (1 new loop on needle)
4. Wrap working yarn around needle point (2 new loops on needle)
5. Lift first loop over second loop and off the needle: 1 loop remains, this is one stitch cast-on

Repeat steps 1-5 until you have cast on the desired number of stitches. Pull on the yarn end to close the circle up to a tiny spot in the centre of the work.

provisional cast-on (crochet chain method):
Using waste yarn, crochet a chain a few sts longer than you plan to cast on. With knitting needles and working yarn, insert needle under back bump of last crochet chain stitch. Yarn over and pull up a stitch. Continue along crochet chain, creating as many sts as required. To 'unpick' the provisional cast on, unfasten the end and it will 'unzip', leaving live sts ready to be worked.

put stitches on hold:
Instead of binding off, thread a piece of waste yarn through the live stitches, so they don't unravel, and then remove the needles.

short row shaping:
To work short rows, you knit part of the way through a row, then stop and turn around before the end. Work as pattern specifies to the point where it says 'w&t' or 'wrap and turn'. This involves wrapping the working yarn around the next (unworked) stitch; bring yarn to front, slip next stitch from LH to RH needle, bring yarn to back, slip stitch back from RH to LH needle, then turn work. Proceed to work back in opposite direction. When the pattern says 'pick up wraps' this means you will work the wrap together (k2tog or p2tog) with the stitch it is wrapped around.

substituting yarns:
So much love and time goes into your knits, so spend the money on quality materials for best results. We recommend wool because is very forgiving (stretchy), can be blocked to adjust size, and makes for beautiful projects. For easy care we suggest machine-washable wools. Sock yarns are particularly well-suited to projects intended for babies; if held double a sock yarn can substitute for a worsted / aran weight yarn.

pinhole cast on

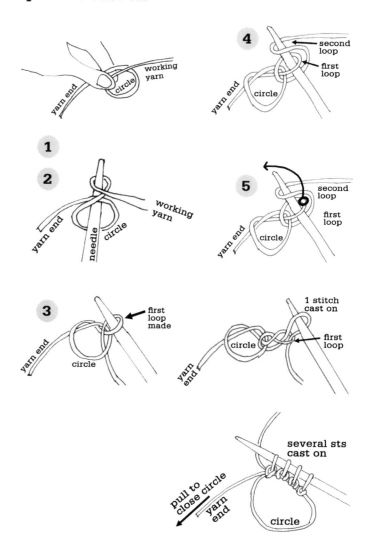

thanks!

This collection came together gradually, with the help of friends, family, and the contributions of many like-minded crafters.

Alexa (aka the best business partner ever) ::: thank you so much for supporting me as I knit thousands of yards of lace, and for making adorable 'wee versions' of the designs.

John ::: thank you for being loving and supportive and always believing in me during my moments of doubt.

The Dyers ::: thank you for contributing yarn, encouragement, and confidence to this project. It has been amazing to work with such gifted artisans.

The Knitters ::: thank you to our generous customers and yarn shops, and to Ravelry.com for creating such an amazing online community.

Other Tin Can Knits patterns you may enjoy :::

rosebud   **gramps**   **photosynthesis**   **stag scarf**   **waffles**

drift   **snowflake**   **dogwood**   **antler**   **lumberjack**

Edinburgh Castle

orrent

hipster

antler

pop blanket

sitka spruce

ons gate

low tide

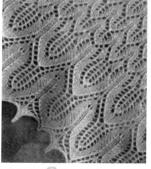

sunflower

tofino surfer

north shore

where?

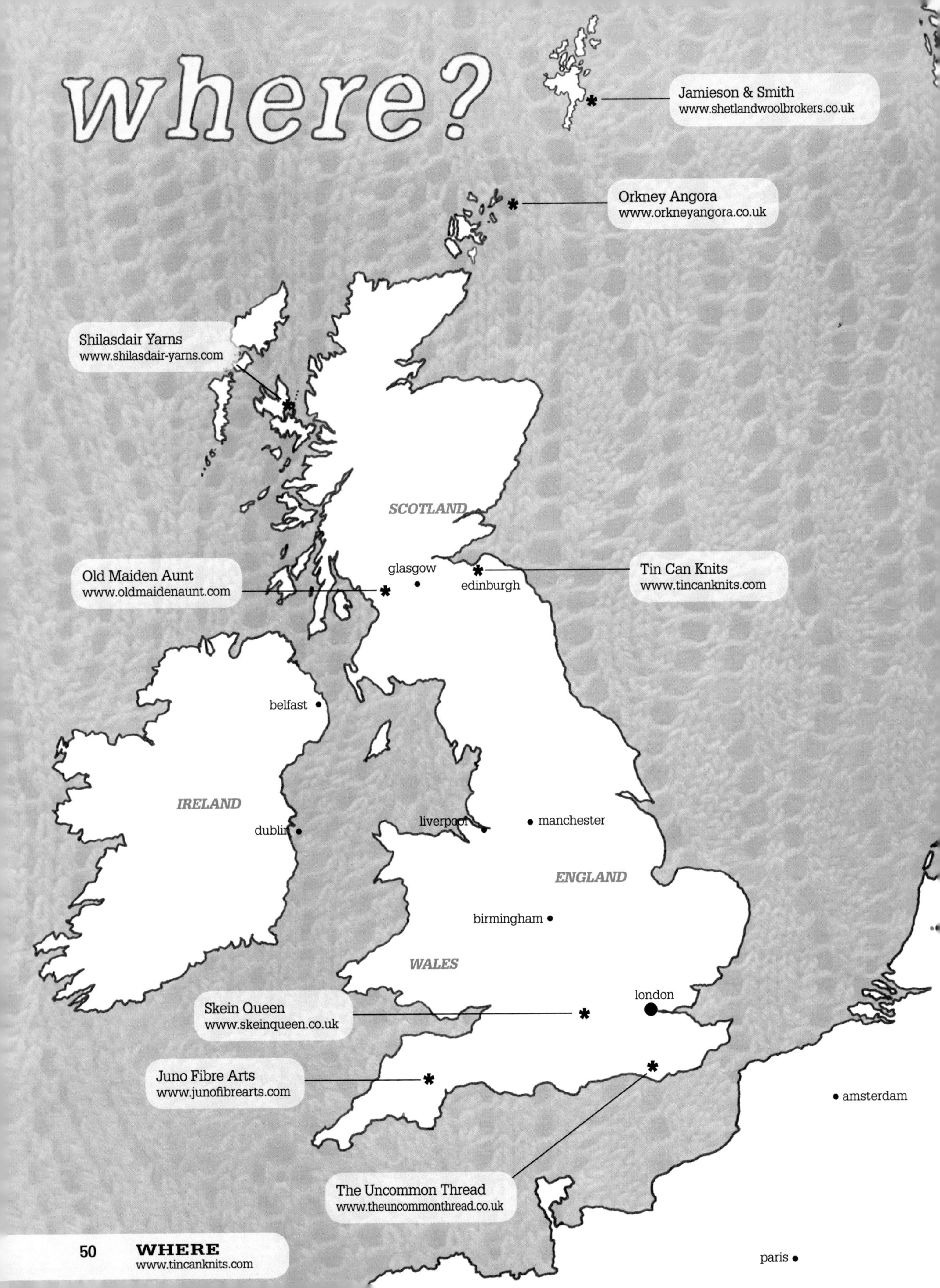

Jamieson & Smith
www.shetlandwoolbrokers.co.uk

*

Orkney Angora
www.orkneyangora.co.uk

*

Shilasdair Yarns
www.shilasdair-yarns.com

*

SCOTLAND

Tin Can Knits
www.tincanknits.com

* glasgow
edinburgh

Old Maiden Aunt
www.oldmaidenaunt.com

*

belfast

IRELAND

liverpool • manchester

dublin

ENGLAND

birmingham

WALES

london

Skein Queen
www.skeinqueen.co.uk

*

Juno Fibre Arts
www.junofibrearts.com

*

*

• amsterdam

The Uncommon Thread
www.theuncommonthread.co.uk

paris •